# A Resume` of

# A

# Desperate

# Woman

I0424840

## And other writings!

## Valerie Miller
## Simpson

"A Resume` of a Desperate Woman"
Written and Published by Valerie Miller
With All Rights
Copyrighted ©May 2010 in U.S Library of Congress
ISBN- 978-1456592103
Images: My beautiful daughter Symantha Miller
Other Public Domain pictures

References
Biblical References
*King James Bible
*New Living Translation (©2007)
*International Standard Version©2008
*God's Word® Translation (©1995)
*New International Version ©1984
*Amplified Bible;
 "Scripture quotations taken from the Amplified® Bible,
Copyright © 1954, 1958, 1962, 1964, 1965, 1987 by The
Lockman Foundation
Used by permission." (www.Lockman.org)

# Cover Letter

Do you know that man's mistakes are God's purposes?
Everything you went through; everything that you've
been experiencing is just a set up for your
breakthrough and success!
God oftentimes conceals his plans and secrets and
gives us just enough information to give us faith to
keep us focused to confound the enemy!

1Corinthians 2:8: Which none of the princes of this
world knew: for had they known it, they would not
have crucified the Lord of glory!

God beat him at his own game and all we have to do is
trust God because He has nothing but good in store for
us! For we can only please Him when we have faith in
Him not by our efforts!
Be inspired by these poetic words of wisdom as well as
expressions.

Yours because of Calvary

Valerie Miller

# A Resume' of a Desperate Woman

# CONTENTS

A Resume` of a Desperate Woman

A Resume` of a Desperate Woman

**The past and depression!**

Greetings:
Oftentimes life can throw some cruel monkey wrenches at you. An individual can continue to play the victim card or simply learn from it to earn from it!
Being unemployed for a season forced me to do some soul searching and reflections about decisions and life choices! Information is power it enables one to come out the dog house of desperation into a confident, uncompromising woman!

Introducing:

**Ms. Sally Desperation:** *And check out:*

"A Resume of a Desperate Woman"

# Introducing:
## *Ms. Sally Desperation*

A Fictional Non-Functional Resume` of A Desperate Woman

# Ms. Sally Desperation

14-75 Anything Drive
USA or Anywhere Lane 10000

**Objective: To find anything or anybody to love me, by any means necessary.**

**Low-lights:  Low Self Esteem, Low Self Worth, Loneliness, Baggage issues and Plain ole Desperation**

## Experience

**Wearing My Feelings on My Sleeves: Type of Business (Retail)**
Duties were: Telling a man I met "I love him" although I just met him a week ago, convincing him that I can't live without him; meanwhile I was living before I met him.

**Jealousy Heart Hospital: Type of Business (Mental Hospital)**
Duties were: Wearing seductive, degrading clothing to steal men from innocent women, but when someone else came along with a more sexier body or old age old crept in, guess what, he was gone (Because the law of sowing and reaping still works)

**Buy Him: Type of Business (Retail)**
Duties were: Short changed myself to make a man happy; found out later that he was a player. Handled currency: Although love is not for sale (other than prostitution and escort services) I had to keep him looking good by buying him what he wanted
**Abuse: Type of Business (Work at home)**

Duties were: Receiving verbal, mental and physical domestic violence

**Special skills:** Could have been treated like a princess but compromised. Settled and allowed maltreatment and sometimes in front of my family, friends, furthermore children.

**\*\*This is why I believe I am the most qualified for this position\*\***

## Education
The University of Black Eye and Disrespect
**Masters of a Hard Head Made a Sore behind Degree Received**
*Graduated without honor

The College of Broken Hearts and Life Skills
**A Street B.A in Life Skills Received**
*Graduated at the bottom of class (Skid Row and went through Hell's Kitchen)

The High School of Hard Knocks and Learn the Hard Way
**A General Education in Desperation Received (G.E.D)**

**References:   7 baby daddies ~ 10 years of Therapy ~ Hospital and Credit Card Bills... But Jesus Paid It All *With a testimony that will help millions!***

# The Bouquet

Why settle for being an ordinary flower!
Strive, and obtain confidence to become the
bouquet,
*The complete and total package!*

# Revise your resume with some confidence!

**Evolution**

It's called survival of the fittest for a reason. Most species that have survived are the ones that evolved and became adaptable during the ages.

*Get to know who you are and go from corrections to perfections!*

---

**Become the best you!**

**You are your own scale of 1-10 (every part of you)**

---

Face facts man does look at the outward appearance and people daily read you as a *resume'* from head to toe!

**We live in a materialist world and presentation is essential!**

The saying they will like me as I am does not hold true in every instance; especially if your personal scale rating is low. If you rate yourself a 1, 2, 3 than others will also see and view your ratings and you may get rejected!

Celebrators are open doors for other celebrators, but

misery is no joke. Everyday ask yourself critically where am I on my own personal scale? Sell yourself to yourself. If you are not buying you, don't expect others to buy you either!

---

**Jealousy can be defined as one peeking at someone else's scale of 1-10 to envy them.**

---

It may be their:
- ✓ Personality --work on yours
- ✓ Charm-- work on yours
- ✓ Beauty-- develop yours
- ✓ Style-- find out yours
- ✓ Intelligence — explore the world, read some books do something [LOL]

Like the teacher says during a test "keep your eyes on your own paper don't cheat"! You'll only be short changing yourself.

According to the worlds standards, you may not consider yourself to be Mr. or Miss Universe. **Develop an attitude of so what!** Be like this guy I used to date; his answer to the world was "wow, I look good to me"!

**\*\*Remember:** An individual will never be as good or

bad as another; simply because they will **_never_** be them. Plain and simple even with the plastic surgery and acting lessons; (not knocking either). Trying to become someone else is nothing but a fantasy and a frustrating dream. God has fearfully and wondrously made you. You are His workmanship created unto *good works*. **It is what it is! (Stop hating on you)**

**It doesn't matter whether you are Armani potential or the Bargain discount shopper, work what you got!** Confidence is not just your clothes:

- It's you on the inside being expressed on the outside.
- If you feel worthy of praise on the inside than your outside will demand that!
- It's holding your head up yes, even in the midst of rejection.
- Not feeling guilty to be happy regardless of your outward exterior, race, color, social ethnicity.
- Embracing your beauty whether inner or outward.
- Not waiting for compliments to change your mood.
- You bringing the mood when you enter the room.
- Loving life because you're in it oh yes, being a part of the plan of God!

### Your gifts, and talents

Maybe the very things that will make you shine in life to usher you to your destiny.

### Gifts:

What you are born with, freely given not costing a thing to obtain

### Talents:

You pay the price for talents because it is your gifts that have been processed and developed.

**Either voluntary efforts like school and training to become marketable.**

**Or maybe you were forced like an eagle pushing their young out the nest to fly because it was time to meet the world to come out of the comfort zone.**

Being victimized or experiencing abuse one can learn from it to earn from it. Furthermore, becoming strong and resilient because of trials one day can be used as a tool to help empower the youth as well as strengthen the feeble minded!

**Once labeled as a pitiful damsel in distress now a seasoned instrument to instruct others about the signs or red lights to stop abuse!**

My sister, my brother; you are not worthless: but either under some type of construction/or development. Sometimes life will take a toll on you. Especially having gone through so much hell, it could bring you to the point you're unrecognizable to you and the face or personality being displayed is not the true you! Although the people you recently invited in your life accepted the mediocre version because that is all they've seen (but you know better). You simply either ignored your current state so long or became numb to it because of all the pressures coming from every direction. Life just knocked you up, maybe slapped the smile off your face. *Now you wake up and the coffee isn't smelling so good!*

**Hey, don't be discouraged because you're still alive and not crazy. You know you've got to be in there somewhere.** *Dig deep if you have to in order to pull yourself back into the reality that you knew!* You must realize that it's not just about people not liking you; it's about your confidence and you liking you!

## You do need to be approachable

**Make yourself user:**

Loveable, if you want to be loved

Friendly, especially if you want friends

Wise, if you don't want to appear as an idiot

Respectable, if you don't want to get dissed

**Come out the prison cell of limitations**

No one can see your potential if you keep it secretly locked up.

Drop the sand bags out of the hot air balloon.

Motivate yourself by being your own cheer leader.

*Yeah for me!*

# It's only the cover read on!

Coming to you under cover because that seems to be

the only way that the judgmental read their books!

A hook and a worm to invite someone into their life!

To seize opportunities to be a success, acquire a

husband or even find them a decent wife!

A worldly system that categorizes personal self worth;

The question is how much do you cost?

Will you settle for less or will you become your own

boss…

Not to be controlled or dictated by the worlds'

standards to sell the common sense away that was

given at birth for free!

What about, I gotta be me!

**To the reader:  Keep reading!**

How long do we continue to purchase covers instead

of shopping for content, quality mystery, novels, or

auto-biographies that we actually take the time to read

and understand?

 Is it easier to take the route of speed reading because

of convenience, the easy road and the high demand!

Do we like what we see on the jacket

but find out later that the information inside is

shallow, lacking nicety, moral character a throw away

and you can no longer hack-it

Books are for enjoyment, to educate to arose emotions

our senses, our intellect, to empower!

The cover is there for purpose as an introduction, an

eye catcher, a road sign, *simply mere design!*

# Time Heals All Things

## *For a limited time only!*

Limited time is broken down into seasons, while minutes, days, weeks and finally years to be curved by merciless death,

Seasons came to present change, to relieve and balance life.

"For this, what we call life has come to live in the midst of this limited time"

Its origin was a heavenly dance, a song of celebration, where the party never seized neither the wine refused,

Because in the eternal gathering one never has to keep track of this thing called limited time

This celestial gala was made to last forever but now on time-hold because of this wicked disease called iniquity poisoning the angels and this being called man.

Yet because of the Bright and Morning w**e the sons will one day dance again, sing again, drink new wine together again, causing a perpetual end to this thing called,**

## *For a limited time only!*

# Out with the Old

### That's not my name anymore

Used to be called a fool walking into doors backwards without reading the divine warning signs!

Friends, acquaintances even called me victim when I "Miss Know it all" refused to become educated about the facts of life and the laws of the universal street codes!

But that's not my name anymore because I now read the stop signs of yielding to the left and to the right! Understanding now that every battle not having to fight!

Restlessness, burning the midnight oil, applying all the lesson plans giving by the master teacher because a lesson unlearned is another lesson being repeated!

Eating the bread of sorrow and worrying about tomorrow use to be me, but learning to trust has truly been a remedy!

A past of being weak never took the occasion to think. For an action for the moment equaled a destiny for a lifetime (But God allows [You] turns on an avenue called Purpose)

Yes, he has a plan… got the whole world in his hand….

Yet worthless, failure, ignorant mistakes is not my name any more!  For my name is success, my name is blessed; my name is I can do all things

### *My name is Victory*

**Yes, that's who I am!**

## "A divorce from sin"

He had never been faithful the whole time we wed.
Cheated more than twice even defiling my bed!

Want a hear more of his lame story?
As far as I'm concerned there was no glory!

You see my ex once lived in Heaven committed
eternal treason…

Controlling and conniving for every single reason!

Deceiving me with all his lies, impregnated me to
commit suicide. Burdened me with struggles to the
things I used to fear!
But ain't it good to know
Christ the Lawyer was right there!

He's well known never lost one case, highly
recommended, It's His authority that puts His
enemies in their place!

That famous case Calvary was done on a tree, the
salary there, absolutely free!

And because of those facts he took my place, for
love of mankind, Salvation for the human race!
The Judge signed the order and I'll never be the
same

Sealed at the bottom

*You're Free Now:*

## *"In Jesus Name"*

*(St John 8:36)*

# *There once were two fairy tales*

Once Upon a Time there were two ancient fairy tales in
conflict to get their story out!

You know the two sides that "Father Confusion" told,

### **But then you have the truth**

Yet the real truth is,

Does anyone even care anymore?

To be Isolated a life time in despair anymore

Constantly alone infected by opinions

The viper of cruelty "the old public venom" Victimized
by their cruel mocking.

Casual falsity, Yet even more relevantly shocking,

**This earths a stone-cold lover!**

More ashes for a burnt heart, appearance devoid
unhopeful, ever to recover

Waiting to inhale to make sense of all this insanity,

To: All the sisters, my brothers that call themselves
humanity,

Stolen sentiments, emotions now all this distress,
disconnected from distant relatives.

 Why such a big mess?

What about Forgiveness and how about some Charity.

Come on creation let's finally get some clarity!

**If change doesn't occur, taking sides of who or what we truly prefer!**

Someone's "gonna" keep getting hurt; the wrong decisions, the past and all that dirt! Let's consult with God and his master plan a simple prayer of deliverance **<u>before we all be dammed!</u>**

A Resume` of a Desperate Woman

# *You didn't know me then!*

You didn't know me then so why even try to know me

now.  Never any inspiration not even one single **wow**!

Mocked at, laughed at, served ashes to ashes.  My

worldly reward, 39 cruel painful lashes!

Never took the time to know my story, but now want

to baste in my infinite glory!

My past to you, most unfashionable, all such a bore

but, baby I'm taking you on a short memory tour!

Remember those years I cried in my closet; not given

your precious time, not one ATM deposit.

In-famished for love but often thrown rebuke, neither

hot nor cold.

You still stuck on Luke.

You didn't know me then, why even bother know me

now.

Your precious time was so, so valuable, pompous

attitude you thought most infallible,

When I was needy you just rolled your eyes

Scandalized my name, sowing dirty, incriminating lies!

Beneath your standards so why give me a chance

saying, go on that line and collect your

**Government Food Stamps!**

## A Resume` of a Desperate Woman

This is my day in court to dance and shine because
Judgment Day has such a fine definitive line.

*NO, you cannot know me now, cause you didn't care*

*to know me then!*

## *Real change*

Change for the train, change for the bus

But yet the real change needed is the mindset,

confidence, the ability to trust

The stubborn need a revival just to be reborn...

To, learn how to see to ride on recognizable

opportunities.

Strategically positioned at life's bus stations... spread

out like an Easter hunt across this God given nation!

The socially disadvantage scream it's not fair,

It's not me, I'm not lazy too much imbalance this whole

entire worlds just crazy!

But blame will not put food in the belly; pay the rent or

those bills getting you over some tuff unjust hills...

Stop playing the victim. Stop whining saying you don't

know what to do.  Read the signs...

"To thy own self be true" See it for what it's worth

You are alive so at least try

Most of this you probably already knew!

Cause the only wall stopping advancement and change

that ole fool might just be you!

# The Solution and a purpose

## And the answer is God

God is a mathematical expression

His Love is equal to perfect love minus the dread of
fear...

His peace is the total of tranquility, soundness,
shielding protection while taking away all your
worldly care.

For he doesn't put on you more that you can possibly
bare!

Yet here is a reoccurring problem:

The ordinary, intelligent and rich have even attempted
to solve them.

- Tribulation plus trials, divided by the worldly
  fleshly sins,

Heartache, pains, pressure you to go crazy and give in

Don't forget about the spiritual pollutions

But there is hope a remedy a balance the ultimate
solution:

Crucify, cancel out self yes right in the midst of the test
have faith, surrender is the things that work best!

Respect is the product of grace and peace be multiplied

Because stirring up division, discord will put everyone
in a shipwreck!

Repentance equals turning around 180 degrees
equivalent to leading one to Godly sorrow walking
away from sin!

To change a mind, a life to make a difference

Sharing, caring with others throughout the world we
live in.

He is the axis point on the graph that starts every
genealogy line in time.

And at some extension of the point the line, God will
curve sin to declare that it's finally over…

- For all souls, He says are mine…

The Alpha and the Omega in which all dimensions the
depth, width, lengths and heights of all things that
were extended from.

He calculates this to be his love from above…

The vindicator of the wrongs no matter how long

# A Resume` of a Desperate Woman

Always the greater amongst the always lesser number.

His victories, compensation is enough to make you

dumbfounded think and even wonder!

The highest exponent to contend with

The $B + C = BC$

$A + D = AD$

$BC + AD = ABCD$ of the Bible

To sum it all up God is the answer

# *This is for me!*

Good day to you and to all those that have been totally un-prized and unappreciated

Saluting the world servicing their every single need,

**how may I help me today?**

Would you like to sit or stand or just do nothing but cater to your own desires that have never been met!

All because you sincerely took selflessness to a level of unspeakable heights completely ignoring your own life.

**Amen to me time!**

So, can I do the honor of getting me something to eat or drink?

**Weary, are you?**

Tired of living to be a man pleaser?  Take a break, possibly catch a breath and stay awhile enjoy you a bit!

Because while you were living that life… the me that you used to know lost its meow…becoming a slave, a servant to know no pleasure but to please everybody but me, myself and I!

**Lonely, are you?**

Remembering being home alone waiting for them to phone or just be a friend indeed

To them just another annoying pest much of a life
treated as second best

This is a public announcement for all to hear and see

Let me just clarify something, **Baby it's time now to do
me!**

# *All a misunderstanding!*

He said that he loved me but it was all just a thought a mishap, a total erroneous belief.

They even said that they cared but it was only that they even cared to listen.

Emerging that they wanted to give but it was only two cents of their opinion that even counted, calculated or even amounted plus the three cents to kill the messenger.

Constantly misunderstood; my only guilt was having a heart that could melt the snow off the ground.

Those were my real charges!

Loving, like the sun won't shine, to be normal, not living in pretense that the world really cared!

Because disappointments baby I had my share!

Believing that the world was concrete, solid, uncomplicated yet had to learn the hard way of keeping my business oh yes my affairs to myself!

Not ceasing from dreaming my dreams, but wisely protecting my visions!

Putting every last one of my emotions back on a shelf for later to protect from every single one of my immortal, haters!

A total recall for success, this indeed works best!

Learning from experience to give God my whole heart,

But discretion taught me to give others just a mere

piece of my pie!

# *He loved me on purpose*

I could have died and went to heaven when He first

captured my attention,

But love said not so

Two ships sailing and crossing in the night launching

me to one divine destined flight to elation in hopes to

rapture my soul…

My Prince, my night and shining armor

While even in my mother's womb desolate unsure of

who I Am was, because of mistakes that happened in

the night season,

The midnight hour

**This is where he awarded me the assurance that he**

**yet loved me on purpose…**

It wasn't because the world perceived me as being so

impressive or spectacular, **but I being special to Him**

My Beloved could've left me for a second but put me

right in the category of His first

Because of this I only have eyes for him

Others may have loved me for my gifts, talents and

qualifications of what I can do for them But it was God

alone who loved me on purpose!

# *Anger*
# *And Abuse*

## *Anger alert, watch your speed!*

Many individuals feel that anger or dealing with anger is a race or cultural thing, but anger is really dealing with control similar to:

- A thermometer or
- A speedometer device.

Whether at home or in public setting it should never be attributed to the past, the color of one's skin, gender, or even one's hair color!

**Fits of rage:**

Galatians 5:19-20 New International version

19 The acts of the sinful nature are obvious: sexual immorality, impurity and debauchery; 20 idolatry and witchcraft; hatred, discord, jealousy, **fits of rage,** selfish ambition, dissensions, fractions

These fits continue to dominate particular cultural(s) because of lack of self control or temperance furthermore education. Not only does one need to control the climate of one's children, to prevent them from developing wild and unruly. They also need to teach them how to apply self control by using one's own life style as a prime example!

The Word of God says be ye angry and sin not:

New Living Translation (©2007)
Ephesians 4:26 And "don't sin by letting anger control you." Don't let the sun go down while you are still angry,

So even God knows that sometimes one will get angry; but what an individual needs to do is to monitor how angry they become and place a cap on it!

**Let's use for example:**
If you were driving on the highway and the signs say that the legal speed limit is 55 mph; no matter how in a hurry you maybe or who's right or has the light; if you are driving above the speed limit you can get a traffic

ticket, into a accident harming someone or even killing or hurting yourself!

These rules are enforced by electrical devices or the Law!

This is likewise in the spirit

You "**can**" control your spiritual car yes your (body, your tongue) through your spirit that is subject to God!

Proverbs 25:28

He that [hath] no rule over his own spirit [is like] a city [that is] broken down, [and] without walls.

I heard individuals defend that they cannot help or stop themselves when they get angry or upset, but this is a lie that has been taught!

Hosea 4:6 KJV

My people are destroyed for lack of knowledge: *because thou hast rejected knowledge,….*

**Temperance**

Galatians 5:23 KJV

Meekness, temperance: against such there is no law.

This temperance is a gift that enables one to check oneself and control oneself when an individual feels the rush of adrenaline in their body to do something negative. All because they're angry especially when it might not be that serious!

## Another example

You are having a heated conversation that you choose to take personal.

The other individuals may be still driving 50mph but you allow your emotions to go to 90 or 120mph because of lack of developing self control!

Bring it back down to 55mph by not allowing your emotions to rule you! The scripture says that you can do all things through Christ that strengthens you.

Give it to God don't let what you feel control the wheel to your destiny, get a grip!

## Learn wisdom and focus!

Proverbs 17:28 KJV

Even a fool, when he holdeth his peace, is counted wise: [and] he that shutteth his lips [is esteemed] a man of understanding.

## *Written in black on white*

Got so mad today that I told this piece of paper off!
Can you believe that?

No. You probably think I'm crazy.

**But  write or type,** Nothing like a good ole literary
fight!

Gave Mr. White a piece of my mind, to the point
that there was no more room for words to
converse...

Got him real good till he was not the pale
white***##    but black all over his 8X10 stature...

**Making it a complete      knock out...**

Simply just relaxed my hands, steadied my fingers
The rage I once felt,  "guess what"?   It no longer
lingers...

My skillful coolness, does it every time......
From the header to the footer     to the very bottom
line...
Yes, it was an incredible fight...

## *All written in black on white*

## *Stretched beyond limits*

You questioning me what happened to the snap-back?

You should've asked me that during the last trial

when I was going through, one hellified attack.

Because being stretched beyond the limited one can

really get whacked!

For they have said down the years, no matter what she

go through   she keep coming right back!

Through the lack, spiritual smacks, prosperity being

hacked, lies, persecutions piled and packed!

Running for my life as if doing mara –track!

Yet this faith keeps getting stronger… patience

enduring longer.

The carrying of crosses "heavy"  more than one tuff

act,

Especially eating trials "**no**" I'm not talking     some

midday snack

For God has promised, and definitely will not slack …

**These eyes being fixed to Heaven for**

*His most awesome comeback!*

# When the milk gets spoiled watch out!

Parents ought-a know that it is difficult to undo the damage when the milk gets spoiled …

Especially when you leave it out too long…

Sitting on the table waiting for somebody else to do the job of putting it away.

The floor gets dirty when the occupants, the little stranger's that pay no mind, no rent with no concern, that make plenty of cents, yet leave the residue of waste for the maid to pick it up.

But they say she's been off her rocker for years waiting for a prince or somebody to put her back on track.

What they need is a good ole fashioned smack. For all this rebellion is mere child's play not a tough act that anyone wants to follow for; I know this to be a fact.

The more I give the more they take away my *ump!*

My God this feel likes the scraping from the bottom of my blue suede shoes.

Another, load of crap my own children have run me to my knees.

# *Just another angry black girl! (A confession)*

Today was a really bad day and I don't mean hair cause this black girl was looking fly and Goldie Locks had nothing on me.

On the E train with my mom sitting still while assessing the environment, my mom always taught me to dress appropriately because sometimes it could be cold filled with ancient hatred that had nothing to do with me but that day I forgot my under garments of love.

We were separated on our journey not just because of our dispute earlier but because there was only one seat available; so I did the proper thing and she sat down... Continuing to look out of the windows, the tunnels of seemingly endless darkness until the conductor finally announced W 4th street. Where I connected to my final destination!

All of a sudden there was a altercation on the platform; a woman tripped and fell. I dare not say by who because I grew weary of the rudeness on the NYC Subway system!

**This image of a human being pushed my mother.**

Seeing her pushed into so many unfortunate situations being a single parent, broken hearted, financial ruin dispossessed from her hopes and dreams I just wasn't taking it anymore!

My breaking point, the cappuccino, the camel that broke the horses back.

 I retaliated and inexplicably pushed that woman back. Not saying a word or arguing because I knew that if I spoke I would be labialized as being just another angry black girl.

No one would believe my side of the story so I silently walked away as the woman laying down screamed profanity at me and my mother.

**In my heart, all I could say is God forgive me for being just another angry black girl!**

## *Silent screams*

Even more deafening than the rolling of thunder

As the screams emanate from the debts of the earth....

More than a thousand feet under!

Shrills from the bed chamber while yet in one's

youth...

Abduction in cars

Domesticated pain

Beaten, beaten till nearly in-same

**Unfaithfulness**

The cold unsterilized blade driven in my chest

**Rejection-Infection**

**Heart break**

**Violence, Abuse, Rape, Molestation**

Even at the top of my lungs but not a soul could hear:

Help me, please help me but a silent scream would

only reverberate from the depths of my heart

Where did these screams go?

Dancing in the church houses, often singing, drinking,

at the pubs, from pillar to post, meeting men or women

at the clubs.

Coast to every coast

A Resume` of a Desperate Woman

wasted degrading lives, still no one would dare to
hear!
You hurt me when you touched my innocence, didn't
even think twice when you tampered with my life!
**So, pay close attention and listen to the silence when
you enter a relationship.**
Listen to the silence while on the bus or train,
and when your children rebel or seclude in a shell,
and when you see your neighbors close their doors
their lives and crack open half a smile...
Listen to the silent screams!

# *Can God be guilty of abuse?*

For if God was an abuser than somebody would have to take His kids away, on counts of neglect!

But God is not in the business of abuse neither does he beat his children's brains out to make them sick, poor, unhappy, or to prove a point that he alone is in control. If you have been a victim of any of this I want to declare to you that this is not God!

God does not curse and punish his kids, boiling them in hot water molesting, harassing, or tormenting his children his righteous children....

He has not called his children to wrath nor punishment...but repentance!

Christ has redeemed the believer from every curse, from the system, the Law that did not work!

It was a temporary foster care system.....that kept individuals from perishing in sin only if they follow every part of it until Christ adopted us through Calvary!

It was his blood that finalized and made our adoption legal now we are his children called by his name sons of god!

He gave us his name and his character and we will be just like him "children of love" through the process of soul salvation!

Again, God is not an abuser, *The devil is!*

**Psalm 84:1** For the LORD God is a sun and shield: the LORD will give grace and glory: no good thing will he withhold from them that walk uprightly.

He loves us and he will supply our needs
He reigns and feeds the unjust sons as well as the just!
But the unjust son will meet God as a Judge if he or she doesn't repent from their iniquities and disobedience...
This is the reason you may see individuals that are saved but in sin for years going to Church and leading a double life and still appearing to be blessed

- Because God so loved them

God is not in the cursing business but loving and blessing business (With Loving kindness have I drawn thee)
Faith works by his Love because, God is Love.
In his love there is no fear of punishment

Yet he gives space for repentance including the workers of iniquity!

Even Jezebel had an opportunity to repent according to **Revelation 2:21**

Men and woman want to abuse their bodies and make the wrong choices and say God allowed it!

God is still defending and declaring that you allowed it by ignoring the truth!

They get involved in wrong friendships and relationships and blame God when things go wrong but He always sends a warning before destruction!

Sending signs and impression in their spirits that something is not right in this situation, Yet the rebellious choose to be moved by emotions and feelings that change from moment to moment and day to day!

He warns because he loves us, yet we grieve the Holy Spirit because of lack of trust... (Being suspicious and full of doubt and fear)

*Yet, God continues to Love us!*

**Reader 1 John 4:18 amp version says:**

There is no fear in love {dread does not exist} but full grown (complete, perfect love turns fear out of doors and expels every trace of terror! For fear brings with it the thought of punishment, and (so) he who is afraid has not yet grown into love's completed perfection.

# Don't play with me!

Happiness what in the world is that?

Is it a drug or some type of illegal contraband?

I aint seen that since 1900, no 2000 and never!

They all said that this is my day.

Come on man, don't lie to me and **don't dare play!**

Saying run down, to the altar, get over here quick for
real.

Your blessings are on the way and definitely sealed!

When the fish break the boat I am truly gonna cut you
a deal!

So why I am trying to figure out daily Mr. False

Prophet; where in the world is my next meal!

**Don't play with me!**

I've been burnt before; this aint no "Let's Make Some
Deal"

**Is the Husband, or car behind the box or door!**

God knows I don't want to take this drama
anymore!

And who in the world wants to struggle and be poor,

It's like some type a disease that no one wants to catch.

Like the master and the slave you better go fetch.

Yet, the impoverish will always be here.

## A Resume' of a Desperate Woman

Where? In the midst of struggle!

Having to work overtime and even to do a double, just

to keep one from being in a heap of trouble.

What's up with that?

Mr. Joneses I just cannot keep up, your inflation rate is

way too high!

Difficult to overcome no matter how hard I try…

Kids screaming at my pocketbook Mommy, Daddy;

buy, buy, buy!

So where is the cow, the milk and the bee's with my

honey!

Somebody's playing a cruel game and acting really

funny y'all better loose here and go get my money.

Real quick.

### Don't play with me

Cause I'm tired of ending up with the short end of the

stick!

## *If hating were a crime!*

Cruel as the grave with all those stares counting all

my blessing giving Uncle his share

If hating were a crime lots of folks be dead taking

life for granted step by step they tread...

Swallowed dreams broken promises. This whole

world filled with the doubting Thomas's!

Heaven add some love to all this madness, just to

deal with the hurting people with their rivers of

Sadness!

# Faith and Hope

## Hope is just my life jacket

*Hope is my life jacket to get me to my faith*

*Saints: without faith there is no fellow no friend nor relation in my ship…*

*"It's just a life jacket"*

*Faith gives me that heavenly unction in life to be a success and function,*

*It's my gas in my tank, while driving over trouble waters, I will never sink,*

*Oh yes, my motivation to try, it also adds wings for me to fly.*

*Although hope revives and keeps me alive, but without faith God will never be satisfied,*

*Because hope is just my life jacket to get me to my faith!*

# *Hope will keep you a float!*

Hebrews 11:1 KJV
Now faith is the *substance of things hoped* for the
evidence of things not seen.

Hope and faith are two different things

Hope is to
- Anticipate
- Wish
- Expect or look forward to or someone doing
  something, or happening
- Have a purpose

On the other hand now faith:
Gives substance (solidity) trust, reliance to those things
we anticipate, and wish for

Faith and expectation are linked together
*But expectation is not faith*

*In other words one has to add some faith to the things
they are hoping for…

Now faith is the substance of things hoped for….

**David told his soul to hope thou in the Lord**
*Psalm 42:11*

It's similar to being in the middle of the ocean or
shipwreck. All you have is a life jacket and that is your
only hope to get you to a ship called faith that will
bring you to the dry land of promise.

# A Resume` of a Desperate Woman

Meanwhile Hope will keep you a float with
<u>expectancy,</u>

I *heard someone say "keep hope alive".*

*Hope is all those things that you're are wishing and dreaming
for **but again it is not faith, yet you do need it!***

Hope is like a generator in the midst of a power failure.
It will maintain your life support; it will keep your lights
on; and your heart beating even when the resuscitator
doesn't work. It keeps you in your home when the
landlord or the Judge tries to evict you!

*Hope will keep you from falling and present you faultless, as
well as keep you together during insecure times!*

# *Don't Even Think About Doubting God!*

*Your logic and rationalization has simply nothing to do with believing God Proverbs 3:2 KJV*

- *Trust in the LORD with all your heart and lean not on your own understanding;*

Purpose is making its
Grand
Entrance!
Busting out at the seams;
in our visions, also in our
dreams!
"The Gift"
That's bigger
then you
And even greater than
me!

# Prayer And Salvation

## A letter to all my haters;

To all the ones that have misunderstood, wronged, prayed against, blocked, and mocked me; destroying my character, while scandalizing my name! To all that have judged convincing others to do likewise; assisted in slamming opportunities in my face just because I didn't meet your outward qualifications!

I love you and forgive you, simply because God loves you,

### And one more thing

Thank you, for all you put me through because without you I wouldn't be the strong me today!

# *A confession of an intercessor*

To all concerned I must confess, the reason why I
went through was all a test!
Seasons of disappointments and nights of
weeping, because the (gifting) of God is not for
selfish keeping!


Rejected, misunderstood it was all a test.
Travailing in the spirit to suppress my own flesh.


Put down, let down, while caring for the flock
Made a public spectacle of, yes viciously mocked.


Eating much humble pie, respected as invisible,
personal pains made me feel most miserable…
The nights: I prayed and stayed up late burdened
to change a hopeless fate!
Devising a plan to see someone else smile,
compassion empowered to make their life
worthwhile.
Oh, My Lord I went through Hell!

Got hundreds of stories without time to tell…

Still giving God a total yes,

**<u>A long with a desire to see someone else be</u>**

**<u>Blessed!</u>**

# *Being brought to you by the following*

*This program has been paid for the by following*

*sponsor; the makers of the Grace and Truth Foundation.*

*The author, the refiner also known as our Faith!*

*Who receives no endorsement of the flesh, including*

*emotional, intellectual, gifting, beauty, lastly efforts…*

*other than credits of the heart!*

*Believing now what was spoken then!*

> *There is no make-up or play- acting…only the special*
>
> *cast of wake-up and change one's mind life editing*
>
> *production…*
>
> *Whose ultimate purpose for design is that one will*
>
> *repent while there is still ample time!*
>
> *For this continuous broadcast is being brought to you*
>
> *by Salvation and Deliverance of The Lord and Savoir.*
>
> *Jesus Christ!*

# *Keep Christ in Christmas*

If Christ is in Christmas than why think just about your selves!

Making plans, Santa demands but inwardly secluding the Son on a shelf!

Not about the rush and dashing through the snow the foolish spending and where does all your money go!

Sleigh bells ringing, the annoying elves singing ho, ho, ho because we got all your dough!

If Christ was in your Christmas, you would remember the purpose and the plan to redeem you from your sin and the gift of Salvation.

Peace on earth good will to all throughout the Land!

# *This is my plea from the man that hung on Calvary's tree!*

Merely mention that you want to be preacher seems
like a curse. Put on collar but make it go in reverse…
Purposely stepping on toes,
Abusing the flock with some hard hit blows ….
Yet, the way of truth, compassion, holiness so very few
choose.

**They done ran my Lords name down by twisting the
truth,** distorted interpretations books of Genesis,
Revelation and do you remember Ruth.
Cruel rejection, fleecing the flock, hearts torn in pain
this is utterly insane.
Shock, after shock why is Gods' name being constantly
mocked?
The prey of the compromising righteous are: God make
me a star prosper me in this land let my name go very
far!
But what about the souls that the devil and hell has
stole?
**Running my Lords name down**
Yes, the city the country done in every single town

**Wake up Church,**

Iniquities being everywhere so …repent from these crimes…..

At the entrance the inferno region a-waits counting interest, with multiple fines….

**This is my plea from the man that hung on Calvary's tree.**

**From the pulpit to the door, the wealthy rich, to the suffering poor, hey do I need to say**

**any-more!**

**His Love expressed was simply divine just**

**To save your soul from doing some hard show-nuff hard eternal time!.**

## The truth

Similar to indelible ink that just won't go away,

no matter how many attempts to white wash,

it won't come clean from the facts and never be

erased!

 Hit it; swat it, because you can't kill it.

Come on I dare you to try to pluck it up, for its roots

are wrapped around a **Rock of Gibraltar.**

Go for it blow on it with all your hot air.

 For the wind that you bluster is nothing but

common fear!

This can only mean the truth that can't

continuously be ignored. cause He is unshakeable

ain't going no-where!

# Patience And Waiting

## A bride's maid ain't getting no rice

Eating lies never makes one wise.

Genuine holiness truly comes with a price!

A constant struggle never a dream of my passion,

single urges, drives of life's presented fashions…

Insanity, desires tempting the soul,

Mysteries appeared hidden the world is so cold.

Preacher, preacher; please pass me some tissues,

Lord help me deal with these promiscuous issues!

Right now a bride's maid ain't getting no rice…

Fornication still sin, so one better think twice!

Who can be kept, because even Jesus wept?

A vow a sacrifice the price one has to pay,

This virtuous life ain't no roll in the hay!

Not to get frustrated or neither be dismayed the

solution for this is that one watch and pray!

*My fleshly battle, now a victorious fight,*

*To prove to the world that holiness is still right!*

# *To the remnants of flowers waiting!*

Wells of Happiness everywhere but not a single drop to drink.

Watching others feast and celebrate while longing for a slice of contentment.

Favor not fair so who really cares; it's just a spiritual strip poker game where earthlings can use another excuse to be cruel and lame enjoying plenty while sipping on fame.

The most nasty attitudes with no moral shame.

Yet the true are still spectators of questionable pleasure not willing to compromise the trash only treasures.

Preserved with the remnants of flowers of faith yes, steadfast even the maids of yesterday still beautifully, gracefully, embracing their promised dreams

**Because God said it is still so!.**

# It's a
# Lust Thing!

**Living holy while waiting for Mister or Mrs. Right**
Yes people, it is do/able without the slipping and

sliding!

It's not just a message but something God said can be

done regardless of what the media, and television,

subliminally advertises. Furthermore, despite what the

religious folks preach when convenient!

Marriage is a gift so is celibacy therefore learn to

embrace your gift!

Many struggle and make poor choices like myself in

the past because of the evil desire called lust.

We live to suppress the lustful spirit instead of living to

give God glory!


What is lust:

- Any evil deadly desire, or sensual, fleshly craving
  that operates by the working of the flesh. Galatians
  5:19-21

Jesus also spoke about this:

John 14:30 KJV

[30]Hereafter I will not talk much with you: <u>for the prince of this world cometh, and hath nothing in me.</u>
Find what in him? The evil desire,
*Jesus was tempted in every way and no sin no iniquity <u>no lust</u> was found in him.*

Hebrews 4:15 New Living Translation
This High Priest of ours understands our weaknesses, for he confronted all of the same tests that we face, yet he did not sin.

**He past every test and there was no secret evil desire in him waiting to be conceived no not at all!**

James 1:15 **International standard version**
When that desire becomes pregnant, it gives birth to sin; and when that sin grows up, it gives birth to death.

Reader it wasn't just about sex, lying, stealing, cursing etc. Satan was looking for something (lust) the evil desire.

Satan came to tempt us through our own (lust)

Jesus never got pregnant to sin because there was no lust in him.

Lust is also like a Magnet that attracts only metal

***Where there is no lust there is no temptation.

Satan receives victory when he uses vehicles like the media, music, wrong friend choices.

The telephone is also used as a Spiritual IV Needle to contaminate and transfer his fowl spirits. (Check out my Book "Issues and Your Tissues" for more information concerning this topic)

Because of this evil deadly desire countless men and women marry because of force! Many feel that if they don't marry quickly they will fall. (Yes, from the leaders to the door). But what if you don't have to fall and struggle, or even masturbate?  What if there is a way to live victoriously without fornicating or committing adultery?  Ignorant years went by until I began to receive revelation in this area. Oh yes, I wish I knew years ago, what I knew now!

We are taught in society that we are helpless and without power, But that's a lie!

Gods word says in James 4:7 Resist the devil…

But if you have already have become a victim

- God can purge or clean his floor Matthew 3:12
- **Matthew 15:13** But he answered and said, Every plant, which my heavenly Father hath not planted, shall be rooted up.

Ask the Lord to remove the evil desires!

# The Past
# And Depression

## *Getting free from depression today*

One of the major spirits that is affecting mankind is the spirit of heaviness known as spiritual depression.

This spirit is being released on mankind more now than ever. It's in the air and it transfers through the walls, telephone, music, and television. You find it in schools, work places, families, churches etc.

Having suffered from spiritual depression for many years, in addition to interviewing others has supplied me with some insight to recognize signs.

---

**Spiritual depression is a thick heaviness, a dark cloud that positions itself on individuals. It becomes a part of their aura bringing the blues, sadness, loneliness, and hopelessness. One may feel tired frequently as well as Heaviness upon the neck Isaiah 52:2

---

During the years I've seen many individuals so bound up it appeared as if they were in a trance.

If the person doesn't resist but chooses to entertain it, they will fall deeper and deeper into its clutches. Eventually their strength and will to fight becomes absolutely exhausted. Satan will even make up things or blow up situations in their mind to the extreme that they might say *why bother with life let me die!*

The appetite is influenced. The sufferer may either overeat or become anorexic. Everyone anorexic is not trying to lose weight neither is afraid of food.

Individuals under attack may feel caught off guard. Under a strong delusion or deception persuaded by the enemy's overwhelming hopeless lies. A suggestion is to be prepared when he returns by having a plan of action in between attacks.

**Stop pretending like you have amnesia when temptation knocks!**

Open up your big mouth with the confession of your faith. Tell those imps tormenting you, frustrating you that I place you under arrest by the Power of the Holy Ghost. I will not let you use my body or do that to me again. Glory!

### *Prayer and Confession*

Father; in the name of Jesus I thank you for this day. I am blessed and highly favored. I thank you for your provision, and protection body, mind, soul and spirit. More than anything lord I thank you that you have delivered me from the powers of darkness!

# *"Reflections of past emotions"*

Watching the Good News from des cruel wooden

pews.

Reminiscing of times, I've been such a fool.

Blindness and Ignorance was my bliss yet many

years' opportunities simply missed.

Body and mind gone through much hell heart

pressed down in this emotional shell.

Did some time on a shelf…like fine wine

Wondering in life will I ever shine!

Nights of pain, memories of shame…cellmate (self)

beat down with… blame

Given Master key for life's dreadful dungeons

Forgetting about mistakes and life's awful plunges.

Releasing my past the most difficult task

But ain't it a blessing to be free, yes free Lord at

last!

## *Tomorrow*

Oh my Go---d it hurts this ruthless journey of rejection
misunderstanding, a cross of burdens that even the
worst shouldn't have to bear.

**Is this how it's supposed to be?** Disrespect, Heart
heavy,    aching everyday    watching others smile,
whereas pretending   greeting the inhabitants as if I'm
there with them in their so called Happy land Life
Amusement park.

**Only I'm being ridden, a personal Ferris wheel    over
and over, and over. again
The same old drama,**

Experiencing brief periods on the top later fixated on
the bottom   as if there were some type of mechanical
error in administration.

Either the breaks not working properly (or just couldn't
find one)   Funny thing though I know I've seen them
same breaks work for others on bumper car journeys
Inside the scary houses the Merry Go Round of twisted
destiny

Hmm, okay the switch is in operation again

**Gliding through the air without the weeee... Got to get a grip It's only me. Going through the motions Driven by sorrows.**

Master please end this confusion... a seasonal ticket paid for by the adversary. The souls he borrowed for the orchestration of his delusion. How long do I come down from this excursion of insanity. Yearning for visions of rapture for all humanity fulfillment of purpose not just another ride in the park but an opportunity to make a positive mark...

## *Tomorrow*

# *Acceptance*

## **Trust**

How can two agree when the one victimized constantly
views through the windows of doubt...and suspicion?
Believing more in the lust, the evil desire...that drives
individuals,
Harassingly dictating negativity in dreams and in
visions
Whispering, I still can't Trust you.
Was it because of the popular magician trick?
The table
The fine serving dishes
A silky cloth
The wine
The fictitious candles of hope
All a remainder of what was left.
After the devastation.
Pulled apart by memories of the episode in my mind
being played over and over again.  Thinking,

## A Resume` of a Desperate Woman

I should have stopped him… I should have stopped
him…

From breaking every intricate part of my heart

Yet I still waited for him

Nine years of an emotional hell!

# *Then life happened*

When I was a little girl I dreamed that I would always
smile and sing the songs of skip to my Lou my darling
Remembering good ole Mary and her little white
fleeced lamb that followed her throughout her destiny
**But then life happened to me**
London bridges not only fell but began to blow up and
burn down all over town
Because of the wrong choices
Especially the day when I met Bingo from next door…
down the block
He was more than just a nursery rock
He became my tic toc, tic toc
Lord it was time to get a lock on my morals and
integrity!
**Because real life began to happen the first time he
slapped the innocence off my face**
Placing me in literal dog house of brokenness!
Left me stranded on one leg fortunately the right one
because that was all that was left.  Pushed me till my
belly skidded on the ice braising the once soft flesh of
yesterday's youthfulness nearly aborted dreams

# A Resume` of a Desperate Woman

Skeletons of my past the abuse still in the closet
screaming, kicking to come out and expose the life that
I once foolishly choose…

But silenced because society said don't complain
because we don't want to hear your pain….

Raccoon eyes the fossils from nights of anguish….

Loneliness, raping my soul. Pipe dreams of crawling
into one large hole and the night-mares oh yes the
living nightmares to finally eternally vanquish …

**But one day I woke up, ultimately grew up to like me,
to say to the world no more, to slam every un-
productive door, to embrace life and all that it has in
store.**

**To blow the horn, a trumpet to say to the world:**

**So, what we've been abused and so what we've been
irreversibly torn, accepting the verification the facts
that Life does happen get over it, simply just move
on!**

# *The final chapter*

Woke up this morning made a quality decision… packed my boxes while discarding all of my outdated weighty baggage… yes I closed the book not even paying the late fees that connected me with all this drama, for this chapter is finally over …. No evil stares today.  Pressed the elevator button with the up arrow; it was time to move on up to the next level to tread upon and ride upon all the clouds that kept me down. Disabling me from being me, myself and I. Yeah it was me in motion!

Forgetting on purpose to check my mail, told the carrier of bad news that I have relocated unto my destiny, no forwarding address required, chow arrivderci, let the door hit you where the good lord … My past now in a different state no longer the next door neighbor visiting me daily for a cup of Joe to reflect on what hits a nerve or floats their bubble. Drove in my car made a sharp swift curve right into my prolonged future at a golden age fed up of being coached whether I like my eggs fried, over easy or simply just poached.

Countless years to get to this stage, but made my entrance arriving on time. Coming to this conclusion it's over the final chapter, **how to say goodbye to a broken heart!**

# Dealing with spiritual baggage

You may seem happy now because of your career, your husband, or the ability to go shopping to forget about the wrongs done to you. Even as you live irresponsibly or put makeup on to cover the abuse and years of pain or scars, are you hiding behind all of this? **To the reader:** happiness is only based on happenings!

**If one were temporally stripped of position, power, your spouse, wealth, beauty, friend's, reputation....** Could you pass a test just to find out if you are truly healed or delivered or even <u>like yourself!</u> Or is it the <u>things</u> that are honestly making you and keeping you all together?

*What would the results be from this test?*

Spiritual baggage can be defined as trust issues, un-forgiveness, yesterday's manna, old ways of doing things and more!

**God wants to do a new thing to give new results that He may be glorified.**

*Release your Baggage today...*

**Isaiah 43:18-19 KJV**

Remember not the former things neither consider the things of old. 19 Behold I will do a new thing, now it shall spring forth; shall ye not know it? I will even make a way in the wilderness, and rivers in the desert.

During the years, I heard many Rhema Words that the Lord is going to bring restoration to my life. Reflecting on the old manna, I would hold God as if he was my prisoner or hostage to my old way of doing things. It was impossible during that time to allow him complete access in me because of my misfortunes.

**Restoration**

Now there are different meanings to restoration one is having something old and using modern technology to restore as close as possible to the original state. Examples might be: an old landmark building, antique jewelry, a photograph, music from an old 45 and 33 record LPs.

Another meaning is to get back, fill up like a store or stock room with new material being marketable for today.

God wants to replenish, restore, restock, and refill our lives with new material. The reason is, what worked in the 70's, 80's, or 90's or even last year is not required for the present. Because God is awesome, He wants us to be in awe of or [wow] of Him bringing us out.

**Trust Issues**

Spiritual baggage can also be trust issues. Everyone you confided or believed in has hurt you and let you down. Now you're fed up to the point that you're unable to trust anyone including God. You repel even the good away from you!

A person with trust issues is often paranoid, critical, fault finding, and judgmental. It is difficult for God to operate through them because faith, hope, trust, as well as believing are closely correlated.

The more resentful, hateful and bitter they become the more they hinder their own faith from operating. The problem is not God but the individual with trust issues. They continue to encircle a wilderness of un-forgiveness.

## How can you mend a broken heart?

There was a song out in the seventies by a popular R &B singer, "How can you mend a broken heart"? I can give you that answer right now. Let the Lord Jesus Christ break it all over again.

According to Ecclesiastics 3 it speaks about there is a time for everything a time to be broken and a time to heal.

When an individual receives an injury like a broken bone, in order for that bone to heal properly it has to be set in a cast in order for it to grow properly if not it will grow and become deformed. The few weeks or months of discomfort will produce a healing that will last a life time. Likewise, even with an individual with a broken heart. God will allow the individual to go through whatever is needed in order for a healing to take place. Oh yes the Lord can heal instantaneously but if a person does not have the knowledge to maintain their deliverance to keep it from happening again it will just continue to reoccur. Tribulation works Experience and knowledge to keep you from falling for the same thing!

# *The funeral*

Recalling for the record:

At 11:59 pm Last night there was a death

No one called the police because somebody finally took authority!

The funeral was approximately sometime after the mourning!

The eulogizers didn't speak long because there weren't too many good things to say!

But at the grave site,

I buried my yesterday

For 20 years to 30 years I lived in, and basted in the past...

Grieving mistakes,

Abusers, lovers, who wore all types of masks, a pity they never did last!

Yet it was a quiet ceremony because we already rained and complained,

Wailed, bawled in a corner down through the ages

You see the condition was acute and the will to live was in the terminal stages!

There was no other remedy but to pull the plug.

No more bleeding Issues,

## A Resume` of a Desperate Woman

Not one more bag to lug!

Leaving a message to the world:

about afflictions, abuse, and pain.

Finally, behind me with nothing to gain!

Hear from experience my persuasive voice

Because on the contrary you do have a choice!

Stop viewing yourself victimized, worthless and low…

**Trust Your God and Let all that stuff go!**

# *Forget about it!*
# *Learning how to forgive*

For many know that un-forgiveness is one of the greatest obstacles that has been in the way for receiving and maintaining a complete deliverance. A big door for depression, oppression, as well as fear to enter!

<u>Resentment</u>

Individuals viewing through the eyes of resentment are influenced by their un-forgiving heart from yesterdays hurts...

*Their thoughts and choices are contaminated with negative venom!*

They often hold grudges and find it difficult to release the individuals that have wronged them. *Unfortunately some just do not know how!*

One Friday evening during a Bible study in my home a question came up. "When you forgive a person do you have to forget"?

Answer: Although it may be difficult to get over what was done to you. I know for a fact that you can get past the memory and change how you respond to the individual(s) that have offended you with love.

In searching in the thesaurus, the meanings for resentment, *animosity and ill-will* were words that surfaced.

**Animosity:** is someone holding a grudge.

It is the baggage that individuals continue to retain even after they so called forgave their enemies or (maybe didn't forgive in the first place).

**True forgiveness involves dropping:** the bad feelings, the emotions, bad thoughts that one has; preserved for the one(s) that have wronged them. Oftentimes used later as a weapon to destroy the person's character. Getting what one would call downright even using devices like words even slander that sometimes are difficult or even impossible to take back!

The only compensation one gets is bitter not better!

**The force behind un-forgiveness is (bitterness).**

It feels like an unshakable unquenchable driving force that makes one compelled to react in order to get even. Furthermore an emotional rush to watch someone else suffer pain or misfortunes (your enemy, your family member, your coworker, your boss, your long time friend)

*Now (you) the victim hurt in the past, maltreated has now become the evil sinister.*

**All because the harboring of grudges…**

<u>Ill Will</u>: Is having a sick will towards the person that has offended you. Because an unforgiving heart is a heart that is sick, unable to operate in perfect love. *In other words one is wishing evil on the individuals, because of the contamination!*

***God desires us to walk in love and bless those who hurt us and wrongfully use us.***

**But how do we release un-forgiveness?**

**Romans 12:19 amp**

*Beloved, never avenge yourself, but leave the way open for [Gods] wrath;....*

*.....for it is written, Vengeance is Mine, I will repay (requite) says the lord.*

The word *[repay] here* means: compensate like workers compensation for getting hurt on the job. *You were hurt living on the earth that belongs to God and He alone will compensate you for the injury!*

*Romans 12:21 amp*

*Do no not let yourselves be overcome by evil, but overcome (master) evil with good.*

- **Get out of the judgment chambers!**

*Math 7:1 amp*

*Do Not Judge and criticize and condemn others, so that you may not be judged and criticized and condemned yourselves.*

Stop waiting for a judgment or revenge for your losses and hurts. Get off the judgment seat let God be God!

- **Drop it, give up resentment and acquit the one offending you!**

Luke 6:37-38 Amp

37 Judge not [neither pronouncing judgment nor subjecting to censure]. And you will not be judged, do not condemn and pronounce guilty; and you will not be condemned and pronounced guilty; acquit and forgive and release (give up resentment, let it drop), and you will be acquitted forgiven and released.

Ephesians 4:26 KJV

Be ye angry, and sin not let not the sun go down upon your *wrath.*

To keep from responding to your hurts the remedy is to submit your thoughts, emotions and will to God. Ask him to <u>cleanse</u> you from all unrighteous.

✓ **Now let it go now!**

[Even the feelings of betrayal, anger]

Ask God to forgive you for holding on to it.

Confess that you forgive them, {even if you have to do it more than one hundred times a day.} Romans 10:9.

*If we confess our sins, he is faithful and just to forgive us of our sins and cleanse us from all unrighteousness.*
*I John 1:9 KJV*

*21 Then came Peter to him, and said, Lord, how oft shall my brother sin against me, and I forgive him till seven times? 22 Jesus saith unto him, I say not unto thee, Until seventy times seven. Matthew 18:21-22 KJV*

Even as confession is made unto salvation; confession is also made *rock solid* unto forgiveness.

✓ **Release it to God and walk in love.**

Walking in love does not particularly mean that one is emotionally tied to or even likes the person.

**Let me give you an example:**
While we were in sin God did not like us but he yet loved us. He displayed this love by forgiving, and dying for us.
***Romans 5:7-8 KJV***
*7 For scarcely for a righteous man will one die: yet peradventure for a good man some would even dare to die.*

*8 But God commendeth his love toward*

*us, in that, while we were yet sinners, Christ died for us.*

Love is an action word, a giving word not always a *huggy feely* word. Yet, Christians are empowered as well commanded by Christ to love everyone although they may not necessarily like them.

This love walk is a giving walk, faith walk, as well as choice walk. Because of this one is able to love unconditionally, forgive as well as be a blessing to their enemies.

### Romans 12:20-21 KJV

*Therefore if thine enemy hunger, Feed him; if he thirst, give him drink for in so doing thou shall heap coals of fire on his head. 21 Be not overcome of evil, but overcome evil with good.*

Check points to remember about forgiving the ones that have wronged you or still wronging you.

✓ It's done by faith believing and speaking in the *now*.

✓ Speak forgiveness even when the devil uses the individual that wronged you to provoke you to want to choke the h**l out of them if you could.

- ✓ You may feel weak, but rely on Gods strength and not your temporary emotional status…. In the midst of weakness learn temperance = self control.
- ✓ Keep focused.
- ✓ God will bring you there

*Remember to add kindness with love*
*Loving-kindness= the forgiveness without the attitude*


Often times it can be the individuals in our homes, jobs, community, or even Church

**[There's no hurt like a church hurt].**

<u>**Running away**</u>

Let's be real running is not always the best solution. Eventually you will crash right back into them or a type of the individuals that hurt you.


## *Pray this prayer:*

First of all Lord, forgive me for being angry with you. I forgive my friends, enemies, family as well as church members that have hurt and wronged me. Lord forgive me for holding resentment, grudges, ill will and, judgment over them. Lord you said in your word in Matthew 6:12, 14 if I forgave my debtors of their trust passes you would forgive mine. Lord, forgive me. Release me from others that have grudges, resentment and that are pronouncing judgments against me. Undo and release me from their thoughts, soulish prayers and psychic powers to will to harm me and all that concerns me. Father I truly forgive them now and I will not harbor any animosity in my heart towards them.

Who the son has therefore made free is free indeed. Lord, cleanse my cloudy distorted thinking. Lord, have mercy on me and rebuild my trust and lead me to individuals whom I can trust. Let me just chalk up all what I been through for joy and experience. Thank you, Lord for setting me free.

From this day on I will be an instrument of love and your glory Amen!

*Regrettably you cannot redeem the 2, 5, 10, and 20+ years lost. But if you don't let go you will continue to waste the rest of your precious life…on the same foolishness.*

One of the ways an individual will recognize if they are walking in forgiveness is when they no longer hear the persons that have wronged them constantly in their conversations.

Healing may take time but God does not want individuals hurting others with their tongue during the process.

# *Spiritually And Politically Incorrect!*

## *Flesh points for earthly credit*

Like an infectious contagious disease everywhere. with
no hopes for a cure in the near future

Innocence is long gone… purity is torn between three

lovers, freedom, lust carefree-trust.

It's driven to the north, east, south and even west in

hopes to taint the plain, simple and childhood quest to

be normal Yet in God's eyes He always knows best to

secure the virtuous.

Wickedness everywhere instructing the blameless.

Incarcerating their morals while polluting their

integrity.

It uses to be that I could hear the birds and bees while

observing the messages from sixty, seventy year old

oak trees..

## A Resume` of a Desperate Woman

Now all is chaotic to even hear a message within a seeming sensible message a pity even gray haired wisdom is corrupt....

For them all that is left is flesh points (earthly credit).to serve the belly and not the Higher Calling!

Where are the values? Where is purpose? Is it in the zest for life or in a golden Fendi purse?

**The city cries out where is the measure of my treasure but they'll be none to journey with the dreadful hearse!**

# *Heaven no!*

What I don't wanna hear that wait stuff again…. while

dangling on the petals of life's so called forget me

not's…

The daddy for the momma, the wifey for the check,

The preacher for the power, while babies crying for

sincere milk!

**Every-bodies favorite sit-com drama**

Telling me to sit right there while they enjoy their share

of respect of per--- sonaal greed …. **Don't pay the gas**

**bill simply just let them warm the pews.**

Pleasuring in others bleeding issues, seeds of pain…

with no inkling of remorse or shame nor tissues.

Telling the world to shut the front door, don't dare

complain.

Yet, plenty of money for their belly, but God got their

game!

You know where they're going, Heaven No

# Beauty's only skin deep!

Beauty's only skin deep   Yeah I know that ain't
Right ….

 Is the Blacker the berry the sweeter the juice?

Let's play the color game and you'll get the real
truth…

Watch them in Aisle 10   when they come back do
it  again…

Education, Employment Uncle you should be
shame…

Nationality, Ethnicity questions same ole racial
frame...

In the media this light is hovering,    racism
influence the sin still governing

Little or no progress the world still ain't right

Don't believe me:   Mention Racial-Profiling    the
buzz word still    generates a fight!

# *Living purposely!*

Waiting patiently at Heavens gate
 Praying to God it ain't too Late…

Lived my life in all kind of trouble
searching for a blessing
God: why do others get double

Loving my life but, living in pain
Craziness is everywhere this world seems
insane

Mistakes in my past, rejected simply thrown
out like the trash.

Living on purpose but the train a little late

On my way to destiny forgiveness first my fate

Lost in the wilderness struggling to be found
Echos from heaven "Look Up my child grace
and mercy's ahead the next town"

# *100 invites to 100 parties but not one was my celebration*

Decked the walls… the backgrounds of the best halls…

Danced with the brides the grooms while in their festive mood…

Serenaded to the audience tried my best to keep in tune…

And to a host of preachers I Gave one heck of an amen!

Smiled at their day toasted their future while I myself drank Kool-Aid eating bologna with the little cheese sandwiches…

**100 invites to 100 parties but not one was my celebration!**

# _____ *Resuscitate...*

St John 11: 23 KJV

Jesus saith unto her, Thy brother shall rise again.
**24** Martha saith unto him, I know that he shall rise
again in the resurrection at the last day. **25** Jesus said
unto her, I am the resurrection, and the life: he that
believeth in me, though he were dead, yet shall he
live: **26** And whosoever liveth and believeth in me
shall never die. Believest thou this?

## About resurrection power:

Jesus did not say that he has resurrection power but he
is the resurrection

- The life giving power

And because he is the life given power... we the
believers have access to resurrection power
Because he lives in us!
Jesus came that we may have life and that more
abundantly!
We have life; we can speak life because of the life
empowerment on the inside!

- He came to give us life giving speaking power, the
  ability to resuscitate.

Elisha had this resurrection power

**GOD'S WORD® Translation (©1995)**

**2 Kings 13:2**

- One day some people who were burying a man saw one of these raiding parties. So they quickly put the man into Elisha's tomb. But when the body touched Elisha's bones, the man came back to life and stood up.

<u>Check out Ezekiel also:</u> Ezekiel 37 New International

1 The hand of the LORD was on me, and he brought me out by the Spirit of the LORD and set me in the middle of a valley; it was full of bones. 2 He led me back and forth among them, and I saw a great many bones on the floor of the valley, bones that were very dry. 3 He asked me, "Son of man, can these bones live?"

I said, "Sovereign LORD, you alone know."

4 Then he said to me, "Prophesy to these bones and say to them, 'Dry bones, hear the word of the LORD! 5 This is what the Sovereign LORD says to these bones: I will make breath[a] enter you, and you will come to life. 6 I

will attach tendons to you and make flesh come upon
you and cover you with skin; I will put breath in you,
and you will come to life. Then you will know that I
am the LORD.'"

⁷ So I prophesied as I was commanded. And as I was
prophesying, there was a noise, a rattling sound, and
the bones came together, bone to bone. ⁸ I looked, and
tendons and flesh appeared on them and skin covered
them, but there was no breath in them.

⁹ Then he said to me, "Prophesy to the breath;
prophesy, son of man, and say to it, 'This is what the
Sovereign LORD says: Come, breath, from the four
winds and breathe into these slain, that they may
live.'" ¹⁰ So I prophesied as he commanded me, and
breath entered them; they came to life and stood up on
their feet—a vast army.

This was resurrection power: that Ezekiel spoke of.
The Dry bones
1.  Are also your dead dreams,
2.  Visions,

3. Hopelessness that you feel

4. Resources

5. Lack of Ambition

6. Rhemas Words, the promises that seemed to be forgotten

7. Sickness

8. Miracles that God promised

9. Your Marriage

10. Salvation for your family or friends

These things that died in the wilderness… Are waiting for you the believer the life speaker

to_____Resuscitate back to life…..

# "C.P.R. "Christ please resuscitate!

Cold Blue, Cold Blue I need a C.P.R. Christ please

Resuscitate me from all the Hell that I been through

My Dreams and expectation experienced

obliteration when you the green-eyed monster, cruel

as the grave stole my hope away.

### Christ Please Resuscitate

These were the blue prints giving to me while

sleeping in innocence of desperation

Non-concealment of future success sharing foolishly

with the world my joy.

### C.P.R. Christ Please Resuscitate

My trust run over by a twelve wheeler truck with

the logos carved in red bloody letters abandonment

Needed a blood transfusion with the blood type

A--gape love but there weren't enough able body

donors,

### C.P.R. Christ please Resuscitate

All my life I was convinced that happiness would

cling to me to be my best friend cutting me some

*slack but. He took the knife and stabbed me right in*

*my back.*

*Lies, lies, lies Come on help me before all hope dies*

**C.P.R. Christ Please Resuscitate!**

# A healed soul

## An oasis

**An individual with** self-esteem issues is like
a withering rose in the mist of the desert...
No-one to water
No-one to complement its beautiful silk petals
of yesterday once admired or dreamed of...
now far, far away
So, splendorous and refreshing, now an oasis
of a confident healed soul
A joyous treasure anywhere they journey
Anywhere they go!

# The compass always points north!

The writer in Psalms 121 says: I will lift mine eyes toward the hills from whence cometh my help.....My help cometh from the Lord, which made the heaven and earth.

"The hills are north" So is God!

Years ago before there was modern technology along with the gadgets they have out now, there was a simple compass. If one were going on a trip on their ship, or even a hike; they would count on the compass to get them to their destination. If one were lost the compass would give them hope.

When we don't know what to do and we are in the middle of a spiritual storm, the compass is saying look to God and his Word. Even when one doesn't see a solution in the natural God is saying keep on trusting, keep on speaking the word until you see the dry land of hope and promise...

**My friend, the compass is always pointing north for your break-through!**

# A Resume` of a Desperate Woman

# *About the author*

*A domestic violence survivor from over 30 years ago who has overcome many obstacles including being a single parent now a woman strong in her faith.*

*If you have been blessed by the reading material I am also available for speaking engagements, women's conferences and or/workshops.*

*Please send all inquires and correspondence to my email address: www.godsplan4uminis@aol.com*

*And remember God loves you and He has a Plan 4U*

*Evangelist Valerie Miller Simpson*

*Check out my website:*

*http://www.evangelistvaleriemillersimpson.com/*

*\*\*Need additional copies of this book, you can purchase them at: Amazon, Lulu.com, Barnes an Nobles or have your local bookstore order them today!*

# A Resume` of a Desperate Woman

# A Resume` of a Desperate Woman

www.ingramcontent.com/pod-product-compliance
Lightning Source LLC
Chambersburg PA
CBHW072200280526
45788CB00002B/808